PRAISE FOR RICHARD HOUGH

"a most powerful story"

— *PHILIPPÈ SANDS, AUTHOR OF THE RATLINE
AND EAST WEST STREET*

"accomplished ... succinct, clear and precise story-telling"

— TOBIAS JONES, *AUTHOR OF THE DARK
HEART OF ITALY*

RITA'S WAR

FROM WARTIME ITALY A TRUE STORY OF
RESISTANCE AND HEROISM

RICHARD HOUGH

WEST
BOURNE

For my Dad
Whose encouragement, love and support are
unfailing, even in the most trying of times.
xxx

INTRODUCTION

If you happen to wander off Verona's famous Piazza delle Erbe, up the side street between the medieval *Domus Mercatorum* and the bronze statue representing the symbolic figure of justice that commemorates the victims of a 1914 bombing raid, you will find yourself in Verona's ancient Jewish quarter. The heavy security and the ornate Hebrew writings on the walls will tell you that you have found the city's synagogue. As you look up at the building, you may notice from the street sign that you are standing on Via Rita Rosani.

Should you venture beyond the city centre, to a residential neighbourhood in the northern quarter of Borgo Trento, just before the concrete of the city gives way to suburban villages and the lush vineyards and foothills beyond, you might come across a primary school that bears the same name, but few of its pupils will be able to tell you who Rita Rosani was.

Leaving the city behind you, head north through the sleepy village of Quinzano, to the remote hamlet of Monte Comune. Behind a row of ornamental cypresses, a series of inscribed stones encircle an ageing cenotaph. Etched on the cenotaph is the name Rita Rosani. This is her story.

CHAPTER 1

MONTE COMUNE, VERONA, 17 SEPTEMBER 1944

A dishevelled young woman with short, coppery red hair and a face full of freckles is emerging from a simple stone farmhouse. Her small pale hands clutch a short-barrelled bolt-action Carcano 91 rifle. Attached to the rifle is a small handmade doll.

It's just before dawn on the eve of Rosh Hashanah, the Jewish new year. The two days of Rosh Hashanah usher in the Ten Days of Repentance, which culminate in the fast day of Yom Kippur.

For Jews, it's a time to reflect on the events of the previous year and to seek atonement for their sins.

For the young woman gazing out across the high pastures of Monte Comune, the day of reckoning has come.

She is surrounded.

CHAPTER 2

*L*udwig Rosenzweig was a young Jewish merchant from Veselí nad Moravou, a small town in the disputed territory of Moravia.[1]

Jews are said to have settled in these lands as early as the tenth century. Since then, they have endured hardship and oppression, persecution and exile. In the fourteenth century they were blamed for bringing the Black Death to the region. In 1648, during the Cossack uprising of Bohdan Khmelnytsky, they were massacred, expelled or sold as slaves. In 1744, Maria Theresa, Queen of Austria and Archduchess of Hungary and Bohemia, banished them from her kingdom, sending, not for the first time, long caravans of repressed Israelites into enforced exile.

Despite these centuries of oppression, by the end of the nineteenth century the Jewish community of Moravia represented a significant part of the population, making an important contribution to the cultural, social and economic life of the region. In towns, cities and villages throughout Moravia and Bohemia, Jews had been tolerated, enriching the region's cultural, social and economic life.

2

But a new wave of antisemitism was about to sweep central and eastern Europe. The Dreyfus affair, in which Alfred Dreyfus, a Jewish artillery captain in the French army, was falsely convicted of passing military secrets to the Germans, and the Hilsner scandal of 1899, in which a Bohemian Jew named Leopold Hilsner was accused of murdering a young girl as part of a religious ritual, had once again burdened Jews with the unwelcome cloak of untrustworthy outsider.

Against this backdrop of rising intolerance and persecution, Ludwig Rosenzweig decided to leave his homeland in search of peace and prosperity elsewhere. First, he sought refuge in the thriving seaport of Fiume,[2] in modern day Croatia, then he headed towards the Imperial Free City of Trieste, then part of the vast Austro-Hungarian empire.

DESPITE RISING antisemitism in central and eastern Europe, imperial Trieste was still considered a safe haven for Jewish exiles. For more than 500 years the free port had been under Austrian control, the fourth largest city of the Habsburg empire, behind Vienna, Budapest and Prague. Migrants were drawn to the city for myriad reasons. The streets of the city were generally safe and clean, crime was relatively rare, and Trieste enjoyed a reputation as a tolerant place which upheld that most treasured principle of religious freedom.

Indeed, Trieste was a multi-ethnic, multi-lingual and multi-faith city, a dynamic seaport that attracted what Jan Morris described as 'a polyglot multitude of incomers'.[3] As well as Slovenians, Austrians, Serbians and Hungarians, Germans, Greeks, Czechs, Armenians and Turks had come to Trieste in search of fame or fortune. There were even a few Americans, Egyptians and English. It was one of Europe's most cultivated and enlightened cities, with

3

thriving public libraries, concert halls, theatres and schools. Viennese-style cafés, like the renowned Caffè San Marco (established in 1913), were popular meeting points for intellectuals and writers, and some even served kosher food.

The Jewish community formed a small but integral part of the city's diverse population (in 1910 the Jewish population represented less than 2.5 percent of the overall population) and Jews occupied prominent positions in finance and commerce. In particular, they were key players in the lucrative shipping and insurance industries, Trieste's principal sources of wealth and influence during that period. The port provided Austria's only direct access to the Mediterranean and Trieste was home to some of Europe's biggest shipping and insurance corporations.

Jews were also prominent in the city's chamber of commerce, in its political and media institutions, and in the artistic and intellectual life of the city. Aron Ettore Schmitz, better known by his pen name Italo Svevo, a friend and contemporary of James Joyce, and the poet and novelist Umberto Saba were just two of the important literary figures to emerge from the city's Jewish community in that period. In 1912, the Jewish community celebrated the opening of one of the biggest and most impressive synagogues in Europe, the *Tempio Israelitico di Trieste*.

ARRIVING IN TRIESTE IN 1905, Ludwig Rosenzweig was fortunate enough to have some well-connected acquaintances in the city. His Hungarian uncles owned S. & W. Hoffmann, an important shipping company based in Budapest, with offices throughout central and eastern Europe. Ludwig quickly established himself as a key player in the company's thriving Trieste branch.

But trouble was looming. The political tension between

the Italians in Trieste, the Austrian administration and the Slovenian population had been festering since the middle of the nineteenth century. Between 1891 and 1915, Italian nationalists had dominated the region's political scene, and by 1914, when hostilities erupted between Italy and the Austro-Hungarian empire, Trieste had become an important strategic objective for both sides, as the crisis in the Balkans spiralled into a catastrophic global conflict.

As the Great War dragged on, the citizens of Trieste faced hardship and suffering. In fact, the conflict brought the mercantile city to a virtual standstill. Industrial and construction projects were put on hold and commercial shipping traffic was severely curtailed. Military-aged men were dispatched to the nearby frontline, and the city was almost completely abandoned. Local authority autonomy ceased and a military regime was installed in its place. Between 1915 and 1917, the city was the target of regular aerial bombardment by the Italian air force and suffered a chronic lack of food and supplies. While the black market flourished, poverty and hunger afflicted those not fortunate enough to be able to pay the inflated prices.

THE PEACE, when it finally came, marked a new beginning for the city of Trieste. Italy's boundaries with Austria and Yugoslavia had been one of the most volatile issues during the peace talks. But in this troubled region, the post-war settlement created just as many grievances as it resolved.

In place of a once mighty empire, there now stood disgruntled and fractious nation states. Vittorio Emanuele Orlando, the Italian prime minister, had clung stubbornly to the Allied promises that had enticed the Italians into the war in the first place, namely that Italy would gain large swathes of Austria-Hungary, as well as substantial territory along the

5

Adriatic coastline. But US president Woodrow Wilson rejected what he considered to be Italian brinksmanship. The ensuing diplomatic spat culminated in Orlando storming out of the conference in tears.

Eventually a compromise of sorts was reached and Italy was given Trieste as well parts of Istria and Dalmatia and the Upper Adige as far as the Brenner Pass. But Wilson refused to compromise on Fiume, a province whose hinterland was Yugoslav, but whose port city was coveted by the Italians. The vexed question of the status of Fiume would be a major source of tension for years to come, stoking what controversial Italian poet Gabriele D'Annunzio would call 'la vittoria mutilata' and fuelling the expansionist nationalism from which fascism itself would soon emerge.

IN ANY CASE, the imperial free city of Trieste was now Italian. For the Jewish community of Trieste, the fact that the Italian constitution guaranteed its citizens full religious freedom was a source of some reassurance in these turbulent times.

With some semblance of order restored to the city, Ludwig Rosenzweig, by now more commonly known as Lodovico, looked forward to a renewed period of peace and prosperity. But, approaching his forties, something was missing from his life. In accordance with the customs of the time, Lodovico chose a bride from his home town in Moravia. Rosa Strakosch was just 23-years-old when, in the autumn of 1919, she arrived in Trieste to be married. Within a year, the couple's only child was born. Rita was a lively red-haired girl with a full round face and freckles.

Their family complete, their troubles seemingly behind them, the future looked bright for the Rosenzweigs of Trieste.

CHAPTER 3

$\mathcal{I}$n May 1920, not long before Rita was born, another family of Jewish exiles arrived in Trieste. Like Lodovico fifteen years earlier, the Naglers were fleeing antisemitic persecution.

Schulim Nagler, better known as Salo, was from Sloboda-Rivnyans'ka, a small village in Galicia[1] near Stanisławów,[2] at the foot of the Carpathian mountains. A frontier territory, Galicia was a precarious melting pot of cultures, nationalities and religions.

During the Great War, Stanisławów had twice been occupied and was partially destroyed by the Russians. The town's main synagogue was also targeted. After the war, Galicia's Jews were caught up in the ongoing conflict between Polish and Ukrainian factions, a convenient scapegoat for the frustrations of the warring parties, as a further wave of anti-semitic pogroms engulfed the region.

In 1918, in the nearby town of Lviv,[3] the Jewish quarter was sacked, pillaged and burnt. One official report estimated that 150 Jews had been murdered and 500 shops and businesses destroyed. Similar atrocities were committed at Pinsk and Kielce, leading US President Woodrow Wilson to appoint a commission to investigate antisemitic oppression in the region.

SALO NAGLER WAS FROM A MODEST, not strictly observant Jewish family. He had married well and his wife, Eige Adele Fitzer, known to everyone as Della, was from a hardworking and enterprising family with an expanding network of commercial and economic interests.

In 1920, in common with many other Jews from the region, the couple decided to leave their homeland. Their son Jakob, known to all as 'Kubi', was seven-years-old when the Nagler family arrived in post-war Trieste. With the financial backing of his brothers-in-law, who had well-established business interests in Stanisławów, Vienna and Remscheid (near Dusseldorf), Salo opened a hardware store on via San Nicolò, in the cosmopolitan heart of old Trieste. Like the Rosenzweigs, they too had high hopes for their new life in Italy.

But by 1920 the mood in Trieste had changed. The collapse of the Austro-Hungarian empire and Trieste's annexation to Italy had led to a decline in its economic, cultural and strategic importance. Trieste was no longer the open, cosmopolitan city of the pre-war years, but instead it had become a febrile breeding ground for racial prejudice and nationalistic extremism.

Against this backdrop a new breed of armed Italian ultra-nationalist had begun to prowl the streets of the city. These violent black-shirted squads thrived in the fervid post-war atmosphere and quickly embarked upon a campaign of violence and intimidation that would become a hallmark of their movement, openly threatening and attacking the Austrian and Slovenian communities, who were forbidden from speaking their native language in public. Although the city's Jews were not yet specifically targeted, the mood in Trieste was tense.

CHAPTER 4

*T*he rise of fascism in Trieste was early and rapid. As a politically active community, it was not unusual for Jews to be card carrying members of the *Partito Nazionale Fascista* [the Fascist Party]. In fact, the founder of the first fascist cell in Trieste, war veteran Lieutenant Pietro Jacchia, was Jewish.[1] Early branch meetings were held in the Café degli Specchi and the Sala Dante, both located within a building owned by the Assicurazioni Generali, an insurance company directed by Edgardo Morpurgo, another prominent member of the city's Jewish community.

In May 1920, under the command of local naval officer Ettore Benvenuti, the first fascist squads were mobilised in Trieste. By July 1920, the local fascist association had 14,756 members, constituting the biggest *fascio* in Italy at that time. The following June, the *Avanguardia studentesca triestina*, the student wing of the new fascist movement, was established.

Mussolini himself visited the city on three separate occasions between 1919 and 1921, heaping praise on the local organisation as an example for the rest of Italy to follow. In December 1920, the fascist newspaper *Il popolo di Trieste* was launched, and the elections of 1921 saw a notable affirmation of the fascist candidates, who claimed nearly 45 percent of the popular vote.

Following the March on Rome in late October 1922, various public buildings in the city were, with the tacit approval of the city's authorities, occupied by local *squadristi,* violent fascist squads led by disgruntled veterans of the Great War. A few days later a fascist procession, accompanied by a deployment of cavalry, marched defiantly through the streets of the city. According to renowned local poet Umberto Saba, Trieste was the most fascist city in Italy. Within a week of his audacious advance on Rome, Mussolini was appointed Prime Minister. By 1924, his grip on power in Italy was absolute. The dictatorship had begun.

ALTHOUGH IT ALWAYS HAD AN ANTISEMITIC faction, the fascist party was not, at least in its early years, overtly antisemitic. Trieste, nonetheless, was to be an unfortunate testing ground for the development of some of the regime's most controversial racial policies.

Unlike some of his acquaintances, Rita's father was never a member of the fascist organisation, a stance he justified on the grounds that his interests were economic and commercial rather than political. But, having fled religious persecution and oppression once, he must have recognised the violence and suppression associated with the movement.

Between February and March 1921, the first Italian translation of the Protocols of the Elders of Zion, the fictitious document that underpinned the antisemitic myth of an international Jewish conspiracy, was published, marking the beginning of a new period of tension for Italy's Jewish population. In Tripoli in late August 1923, the fascist authorities launched a punitive expedition against the city's Jewish community. Closer to home, in Padova, a 50-strong squad launched the first known attack on an Italian synagogue in over 50 years.[2]

DESPITE THE FESTERING TENSIONS, the two migrant families lived peacefully and prospered in their adopted hometown, which was by now home to one of the largest and most influential Jewish populations in Italy.

In 1927, the Rosenzweigs applied for Italian citizenship. With a handwritten reference from an influential senator, their application was eventually approved. The following year, in a further sign of their integration into Italian society, the Rosenzweigs officially changed their name to Rosani. The Naglers, meanwhile, lived in a large tenement building near Piazza Garibaldi, a respectable neighbourhood, if not quite as fashionable as the Rosani's apartment on Via Milano.

Over the years, the bond between the two families had grown close. They shared a common background, religion and outlook on life. Although Kubi was seven years older than Rita, they mixed in the same social circles. A photograph of him from the time shows an elegant, dapper and well-heeled young man, with a high receding hair line and round rimmed spectacles, a look that made him appear older than his 26 years. Well-spoken, urbane and aspirational, Kubi had been studying Portuguese and Spanish, perhaps with the intention of starting a new life in South America.

Short and sturdy with curly red hair and freckles, Rita was a vivacious and lively young woman with a healthy disregard for authority and tradition. Like most girls of her age, she had an interest in clothes and fashion and was an avid reader of the weekly lifestyle magazine *Grazia*. She had a certain rebellious streak, painting her nails bright red and smoking the occasional cigarette, even though she knew her mother disapproved. She was a hardworking and diligent student, not without her insecurities, whose dream was to become a teacher.

Although life in Trieste was becoming increasingly volatile, antisemitism was not yet a cause for undue concern and the two families, by now well integrated into Italian society, had no reason to feel at risk. That was all about to change.

CHAPTER 5

*T*hroughout the 1920s and 1930s, Trieste was an important staging post for European Jews fleeing antisemitic persecution. In 1920 more than 2,500 Jews sailed from Trieste to the Americas and over 4,000 left for Palestine, earning the city the nickname the Gateway to Zion. Other European ports were available, but Trieste's facilities, its well-developed rail to sea connections from central Europe and the relatively tolerant attitude of the Italians, made Trieste the favoured route for Jewish emigrants bound for Palestine.

As the situation in central and eastern Europe deteriorated, the flow of migrating Jews intensified. Between 1933 and 1940, over 120,000 Jews passed through the city on their way to Palestine or America. Amongst them, a German-born theoretical physicist named Albert Einstein.

The increasing flow of migrants contributed to an economic boom for the city. Many of those fleeing, though, were impoverished and destitute. In January 1921, the Jewish Consortium had established an Italian Committee of Assistance for Jewish migrants. Trieste, because of the high numbers passing through the port city, was the principal operational base for the organisation. In fact, a system of assistance had been in existence in the city since at least 1908, when Russian refugees escaping pogroms and persecution had required assistance.

When she was old enough, Rita volunteered to help alongside her mother. As Italian Jews, they were, for the time being, insulated from the most direct consequences of the rising tide of antisemitism sweeping the continent. Rita's involvement with the committee of assistance exposed her to the language, culture and politics of her parent's homeland, as well as to the devastating impact of antisemitic ideology.

Between 1920 to 1937 the committee assisted 157,000 emigrants and refugees. Rita's contribution at this point was limited to makings dolls for refugee children as they waited for passage to the new world, but over the years, as the political situation in Italy intensified, her work for the committee would take on greater significance, propelling her towards the clandestine world of people smuggling, gunrunning and armed resistance.

THE FLOW of Jewish migrants through the city did not go unnoticed and coincided with a rising campaign of anti-semitic propaganda emanating from Rome. Claims were made that freemasons in Trieste, guided by a Jewish elite, represented an 'unsolvable problem', while the German consul in Trieste expressed concern that commercial activity in Trieste, including banking, insurance, coffee, tobacco, fruit and wine trading, were under exclusive Jewish control.

In 1933, the Italian Ministry of the Interior, concerned that it was involved in the organisation of anti-fascist activities, instructed the Triestine prefect to investigate the activities of the Jewish committee of assistance. The prefect found that the committee had strictly philanthropic intentions, but promised to maintain careful vigilance of the organisation. At the same time, an article appeared in Mussolini's *Il Popolo d'Italia* claiming that Jews were running Trieste and all the important offices within it, despite representing just two percent of the city's population.

In June 1937, a list was circulated documenting the financial and political influence of Trieste's Jewish population, a propaganda exercise that fed existing notions of a Jewish conspiracy at the heart of the city's political and economic life.

By autumn 1937 overt antisemitism was prevalent throughout Italy. The police and carabinieri considered Jews a threat to public order and fermenters of anti-government activity. Italian Jews were now specifically targeted by fascist propaganda. Minister of State Roberto Farinacci, editor of *Il regime fascista*, a virulent antisemite and long-time proponent of alliance with Germany, published specific charges that the committee of assistance in Trieste was involved in anti-fascist and communist activities, labelling members of the committee dangerous enemies of the regime.

Galeazzo Ciano, Mussolini's son-in-law and Minister for Foreign Affairs, responded to Farinacci's attack by highlighting the commercial benefits of increased traffic from central Europe through Trieste. Regardless of his motivations, Ciano's intervention enabled Jewish emigration to continue through Trieste and undoubtedly saved lives.

While Jews were labelled enemies of the state in the national media, in Trieste local newspapers regularly carried overtly antisemitic features. An unsigned report entitled 'The Semitic Movement in Trieste' cast Jews as members of a predatory and dangerous race.

The Triestine Jewish community's apparent wealth and influence fuelled this rising tide of antisemitism. The

perceived commercial orientation of the city's Jewish population meant that accusations of an international conspiracy
and common stereotypes of greedy, self-serving Jew could be
applied with particular effect.

In fact, the city's Jewish population were of varied back-
grounds and held a diverse range of political views. While
Jews belonging to the working class were relatively few in
number, their presence in the lower-middle or white collar
class was significant. Some of the city's Jewish communities,
including those of Greek origin from Corfu, lived in relative
poverty.

In April 1938, vandals painted the door of a house in the
city with the words *'Juden hinaus* [Jews out], Heil Hitler'. In
August 1938, graffiti scribbled on the walls of the Café Adri-
atico read *'Ebrei è venuta la vostra ora—Abbasso questo caffè!'*
[Jews, your time has come—Down with this café!]. Meanwhile, in Ferrara, a request was made to replace the Jewish
Podestà Renzo Ravenna with a Catholic.[1] While Ravenna
clung on, the message was clear — Jews should not to be
entrusted with public office.

On 22 August 1938, an official nationwide census of
Italy's Jewish population was conducted, a preliminary act of
systemic discrimination that paved the way for the arrests
and deportations that would follow. Questionnaires were
distributed to every family with at least one Jewish member.
The Rosanis had to cut short a family holiday in the mountains to take part in the mandatory survey.

On 18 September 1938, Mussolini once again came to
Trieste, where he delivered a savage attack on Judaism,
describing the religion as an irreconcilable enemy of the
state. He was, however, careful to draw a distinction between
loyal Italian Jews and foreigners. Perusing the media
archives, the language and sentiment that accompanied
Mussolini's visit to Trieste that day is difficult to compre-

hend now, as is the messianic adulation that greeted his arrival. With an increasing sense of loss, bewilderment and fear, the Jewish community braced itself for the onslaught that would inevitably follow Mussolini's ferocious intervention.

THE CONSTANT BARRAGE of antisemitism clearly took its toll on the impressionable young Rita. During this period she often seemed sad and sought out solitude to escape from the turmoil engulfing the city around her. Her parents were so concerned about her behaviour that they tried to persuade her to see a doctor.

The hammer blow came on 17 November 1938. *Regio Decreto Numero 1728*, the most significant of the Italian racial laws, which restricted the rights of Jews in Italy, banned their books and excluded them from public office, schools and higher education. At a stroke, 96 Jewish professors were removed from teaching positions at Italian universities. Jews, even Italian citizens, were banned from owning property, land and business. They were prevented from hiring non-Jewish employees and from working in public administration, educational institutions, banking, insurance, newspapers and publishing. They could no longer join a political party and were expelled from the fascist organisation.[2]

While foreign Jews were to be expelled from the country, between September and October 1938, Mussolini explored the practicalities of revoking the citizenship of all Italian Jews. In the end he had to settle for removing the citizenship rights of those foreigners who had acquired citizenship after 1 January 1919.

Italy's anti-Jewish legislation was now amongst the most draconian in Europe. Though closely modelled on Hitler's racial laws, the measures introduced in 1938 were even harsher than those enshrined in Germany at that time.

For the Rosanis and the Naglers the consequences were immediate and devastating. Not only was their livelihood impaired, they were stripped of their dignity and self-worth. The Naglers, having entered Italy after 1 January 1919, were now classified as foreign Jews and faced the threat of expulsion. Rita was prevented from going to school and forbidden from ever studying at university. All her hopes, dreams and ambitions for the future were crushed. To add insult to injury, she was even expelled from her alpine club.

DURING THE WINTER OF 1938, as the bracing cold *bora* wind whipped through the city, the implementation of the racial laws began to bite. Half of Trieste's native Jewish population fled, forced to use the emigration routes they had created and maintained for others, to begin new lives in Palestine, America, Canada and South America. Families were torn apart. Some had already left, others were desperately trying to secure safe passage from Italy. Each faced its own agonising decision — persevere in an increasingly hostile landscape or abandon everything and flee.

Between 1938 and 1940, when Italy entered the war, more than 25,000 Jews departed Trieste for Palestine. Della's sister, Helene Peller, was amongst those who fled to America. She tried to convince the Naglers to join her, but Kubi was indecisive and Salo resisted. He had already fled anti-semitism oppression once and he was determined not to have to do so again. His shop was his life's work and he continued to hope for a miracle. But for those who stayed behind, it would soon be too late. The noose around Italy's Jewish population was about to get even tighter.

CHAPTER 6

*D*espite the systemic oppression of the Jewish population, daily life in Trieste limped on with some semblance of normality. In the spring of 1939, Rita and Kubi announced their engagement. An arranged marriage of sorts - as was the way of things in those day - but a rare moment of joy amidst the deepening gloom.

The two families exchanged gifts. Rita presented Kubi with one of her handmade dolls. They ate, drank and celebrated together and as they danced Kubi held Rita closer than might, in different circumstances, have been allowed.

In March 1939, just as German troops were marching into Czechoslovakia, the Polish government suddenly decided to revoke the citizenship of those expatriates who, like the Naglers, had migrated from what was then Austrian Galicia. Denied Italian citizenship, Salo, Della and Kubi were now officially stateless. They entered a treacherous bureaucratic limbo, unable to emigrate even if they had wanted to.

By the early summer of 1940, while Churchill was declaring that Britain would never surrender and Mussolini was pondering Italy's participation in the spiralling conflict engulfing the continent, the situation in Trieste deteriorated even further. Emboldened by the wider political situation, squads of young fascists prowled the streets of the city, attacking the British and French consulate as they went. Jews were abused and property, including the synagogue, was targeted.

On 15 June 1940, five days after Italy had declared war on Britain and France, the order was given to intern all foreign and stateless Jews aged between 18 and 60. Salo was amongst the first to be detained. On 23 June, he was taken to the city's notorious Coroneo prison and held in a crowded cell with only a bucket for comfort. For a respectable businessman, whose only wish was to live peacefully in his adopted home-town, his sudden incarceration was a crushing blow.

After spending a few days in the city jail, Salo was trans-ferred 400 kilometres south to the internment camp at Casoli in Abruzzo. Chosen for its remote location, the central Italian region was the site of several internment camps for citizens of hostile nations, including French, British and Poles, as well as Jews, political prisoners and other 'undesirables'.

A week after the imprisonment of his father, Kubi was also arrested. He too was held at Coroneo, where he spent a month behind bars before being transferred to the intern-ment camp at Ferramonti, a malaria-infested region in the southern toe of Italy.

Conditions for the prisoners at Ferramonti were primi-tive, with no running water, sanitation or electricity. As summer temperatures soared to 40 degrees Celsius, a meagre water ration was distributed just twice a day. Under the strict guard of fanatical black-shirts, life at Ferramonti was a far cry from Kubi's comfortable upbringing in pre-war Trieste.

Whilst conditions gradually improved (parcels from family eventually arrived and various recreational activities were also permitted), Kubi was anxious to be reunited with his father at Casoli, where conditions for internees were much more tolerable.

NOT LONG AFTER arriving at Ferramonti, Kubi received his first letter from Rita. It had already been opened by the censor and parts of it had been removed, deleted or expunged. Seeking solitude in which to read her words, Kubi missed the morning distribution of water and had to wait until evening to quench his thirst. Just 24 hours later, he received a second letter from his fiancée. If nothing else, the fascist postal service was efficient.

Throughout his period in detention Rita wrote to Kubi with unfailing regularity. She was curious about his life at the camp, about how he spent his time and whether he had made any friends. She informed him that his father had written to her and that he was desperate for news from his son.

She would describe her daily routine, her studies, her day trips spent bathing or cycling with her friends or listening to music. She described her life as *'noiosa fino all nausea'* [nausea inducing boredom]. Recognising the monotony of her life, she apologised to Kubi — 'this is my life and I can't make it any more interesting when it isn't so.'

During the period of his incarceration, the infrequency of Kubi's replies (he wrote to Rita about once a week) was a recurring source of frustration for Rita, for which she frequently chastised him. Of course, subject to the rules of interment, he was not at liberty to write with any greater frequency.

No doubt conscious of the prying eyes of the censor, Rita's letters seem to lack spontaneity, intimacy and affection. She was often direct and forthright, sometimes even cold. On one occasion, she closed a letter with a simple signature, 'Rita'. When he used the rather formal *'cordiali saluti'* to close one of his letters, Rita was quick to rebuke him in her reply. Their correspondence certainly doesn't seem like the exuberant exchanges of a young couple in love. Perhaps, in the circumstances, that is understandable.

Although Kubi's letters to Rita haven't survived, we know from her responses to him that he was worried about her, about her weight loss and her recurring bouts of depression. He urged her to see a doctor, which she flatly refused. In one letter, dated 21 January 1941, she wrote:

> I'm so tired of living, that in certain moments I don't know what to do with myself. I think that if I died tomorrow, I'd feel a sense of liberation.

It was a dark period for the young couple. Their destiny lay in the hands of powerful forces far beyond their control.

FOR THOSE LEFT behind in Trieste, daily life was a struggle. Della, far from her husband and son, had moved in with the Rosanis. Many of their friends and relatives had fled or had been deported. The synagogue had become the target of increasingly serious attacks. When Rita made it to the temple, she noticed how empty the pews were. But somehow life stumbled on for what remained of the city's Jewish population. Acquaintances were discreetly married, a source of mixed emotions for Rita as her own dreams of marriage now seemed remote. Despite the strain they were all under, the bond between the two families remained strong.

On 13 September 1940, Kubi was transferred from Ferramonti to the internment camp at Casoli, where he was finally reunited with his father. Here, conditions were much better than those he had endured for nearly three months at Ferramonti. Notwithstanding the hardships of wartime life in rural Italy, the internees were relatively well cared for. In fact, when their situation worsened in the winter of 1942/43, Kubi and his father would look back at their time at Casoli with something approaching nostalgia.

Aside from the presence of the four card-carrying fascist guards, there was none of the overt antisemitism that had blighted their lives in recent years in Trieste. In fact, some of the locals began to discreetly open their doors to the cultured and exotic outsiders who had landed in their midst. The internees helped the local children with homework and music lessons and regaled them with stories of exotic faraway lands. In return, the children of the village smuggled fresh eggs and homemade biscuits to the internees, who they grew increasingly fond of.

Despite these small comforts, the misery of internment was taking its toll on Kubi and Salo. On 4 October 1940, it was Rita's turn to try and cheer up Kubi:

> It seems really strange my Kubi that you come and tell me that you've got apathetic and indifferent, you who always says to have high spirits. What's happened to you little dear. It's no good like this. Think dear that you're only 27... one day we'll reconquer this lost time and everything will be better again.

Rita was right to be concerned about Kubi. During the years of fascist oppression there was an alarming spike of suicides in the Jewish community, many cases involving young men. Salo's deteriorating health was another source of concern and his family desperately appealed for his release on compassionate grounds.

On 8 December 1940, a 20-day pass for home leave was

finally granted to allow Salo to oversee the liquidation of his shop, as required by the antisemitic racial laws. Meanwhile, Della had secured maintenance guarantees from relatives in America, who had also agreed to finance the family's passage from Italy. Of course, there were many other barriers to overcome, not least obtaining the necessary travel permits and visas, but flight from Italy now seemed like the Nagler family's best hope of survival.

Aside from the internment of her fiancé and the deepening crisis engulfing the Jewish community, Rita's biggest preoccupation during this period was her studies. Although the racial laws prohibited her from attending school, she had been able to continue her education privately. Despite the strain she was under, she achieved satisfactory grades and, although unable to work in a public school, in late October 1940 she began teaching at the Jewish school in Trieste. In a letter to Kubi, she described her first day in the classroom:

> The girls are really delightful, even the boys aren't bad, in total 22....I don't think being a teacher is the easiest thing in the world. I can't tell you how much patience you need. Lots, and then an incredible imagination, to go on for 4 hours telling story after story in a way that the children don't get bored even for a moment. But there's a girl who makes it all worthwhile. She's a frugolino [a cartoon character of the era] with small, black eyes and a tiny tiny nose, if I could I would smother her with kisses and I think you would too if you could see her.

With a new vocation in life, Rita's mood seemed to lighten. Once more she teased her boyfriend (about his German accent) and looked forward to the days when they would be together again. In one letter she reminded him that in just three weeks she would be twenty. 'What are you going to get me?', she asked him, perhaps with mock enthusiasm. But when her birthday came, it was with a renewed sense of melancholy that she reflected on the milestone: 'Are my best years behind me?', she wondered. 'What does the future hold?'

Rita Rosani (photo credit: CDEC Digital Library)

CHAPTER 7

*S*alo spent Christmas 1940 on home leave in Trieste, leaving Kubi to pass a bleak Christmas alone in Casoli. All too soon though, Salo's home leave came to an end and, his business interests in Trieste wound up, he reluctantly returned to Casoli.

As winter 1940 turned to spring 1941, Salo was informed that he was to be transferred to the internment camp at Castel Frentano, where his wife would be permitted to join him. Kubi, though, was to remain behind at Casoli.

On 12 April 1941, Della left Trieste. She would never see her adopted hometown again. Tired and anxious, she arrived four days later and was once again reunited with her husband. Under armed guard they were taken first to Lanciano, then Archi and finally to Castel Frentano, where they eventually arrived on 7 June.

A photo of Kubi dated 1 June 1941 shows him posing with the camp guards, dressed immaculately in suit and tie and, despite the circumstances, exuding an air of refined entitlement. Separated from his parents by just a few miles,

Kubi begged for permission to see his mother, even if just once a week. His requests were denied.

Desperate to see her son, Della even wrote to Donna Rachele, Mussolini's wife, imploring her to intervene on their behalf.[1] The transfer request was eventually approved, and the family were finally reunited at Castel Frentano on 6 December 1941.

BY THE SUMMER OF 1941, France, Luxembourg, Belgium, Denmark, Greece, Hungary, Norway, the Netherlands, Yugoslavia, Austria, Czechoslovakia, Lithuania, Poland, Serbia, Slovakia and the Ukraine had all been defeated by the Nazi war machine. Much of continental Europe was now under fascist occupation. Across occupied Europe, the star of David armband was a stark symbol of the stigmatisation of a race that would culminate in its near extermination.

By now plans for a 'final solution to the Jewish question' were beginning to take shape.[2] Hitler himself had already publicly declared that the Jews of Europe must be exterminated. The Nazi high command, including Reichsführer Heinrich Himmler and Obergruppenführer Reinhard Heydrich, who as Acting Reich Protector of Bohemia and Moravia was effectively military dictator of the region, enthusiastically embraced the policy, while the Einsatzkommando, Heydrich's paramilitary killing squads, were unleashed to deliver its brutal implementation.

In Oswiecim, a small town in south-west Poland, SS commandant Rudolf Höss, the fanatical commandant of a Nazi concentration camp, had begun to experiment with a cyanide-based pesticide called Zyclon-B. The camp he ran would become better known by its German name — Auschwitz.

Massacres and atrocities in towns, villages and cities

across eastern and central Europe were now commonplace. In Lviv, just a few hours to the north of Stanisławów, where Salo Nagler had grown up, hundreds of Jews were arrested, detained and executed. Polish academics from the two universities in Lviv were rounded up along with their families. They were subsequently beaten to death, killed with a bayonet or hammer, or shot by the mobile killing squads of the Einsatzkommando. On 26 July, Kazimierz Bartel, the former Polish prime minister, became another victim of the Nazi killing squads.

On 2 August, under the guise of 'registering the wealthier class', 800 Stanisławów Poles and Jews were ordered to report to the police. Of those detained, 200 skilled workers were released. The rest were transported to a forest near Pawelce in Poland where they were executed.

On 12 October, 10,000 Jews were herded into Stanisławów's market square for selection. The Einsatzkommando (aided and abetted by local collaborators) escorted the detainees to the Jewish cemetery, where mass graves had already been prepared. At the cemetery the Jews were ordered to show their papers and hand over their valuables. They were then forced onto a walkway suspended above the vast burial pit where they were shot.

The Bloody Sunday massacre, as the atrocity became known, began at noon and continued until nightfall. Whole families were exterminated — mothers and fathers alongside their weeping children. Picnic tables had been laid out with bottles of vodka and sandwiches to sustain the killers. In a single day, in scenes that would be replicated in towns, villages and cities across the region, Stanisławów's Jewish population of between 10,000 and 12,000 was virtually wiped out.

A ghetto was then established at Stanisławów, where Jews from across the region were concentrated before being deported to death camps. On 31 March 1942, on the eve of Passover, several thousand Jews from the Stanisławów ghetto were rounded up, their houses burnt to smoke out any still in hiding. The next day, the remaining survivors were marched to the train station and deported to the extermination camp at Belzec.

On 11 September 1942, the Nazis marked the first day of the Jewish new year by rounding up another 5000 Jews from the Stanisławów ghetto and sending them to Belzec. Many others were killed on the spot. In January 1943, 1,000 Jews were seized and shot and a further 1,500-2,000 were deported to the Janowska camp in Lviv. Those who weren't killed would die of hunger.

On 22 and 23 February, preparations began for the final liquidation of the Stanisławów ghetto. The Einsatzkommando conducted a house-to-house search to flush out any remaining Jews. A few hundred were found and taken to the Jewish cemetery where they were executed with a bullet to the back of the head. Although the ghetto had been liquidated, the security police would continue to scour the area until April, apprehending and executing any Jews still found to be in hiding. Throughout Galicia, between 1941 and 1943, approximately 70,000 Jews were shot and killed. A further 12,000 were deported to the death camps.

It was a similar story in Moravia, the land Lodovico Rosenzweig had fled decades earlier. By October 1941 the deportation of the Moravian Jews to the ghettos of Łódź and Theresienstadt had begun. On Heydrich's orders, the population of Theresienstadt had already been cleared out of their homes to make way for thousands of Jews who would pass through the ghetto on their way to the death camps. Conditions were so bad that by September 1942 almost four thousand detainees had died of starvation.

Between 1941 and 1945, nearly 140,000 Jews were

brought to Theresienstadt. Of these, 33,430 would die in the ghetto, while 86,934 were deported to the extermination camps at Maly Trostenets and Auschwitz. Property stolen from the Jews of Moravia was transported to Prague, where the Nazis planned to open a Museum of the Lost Jewish Race.

NEWS of the atrocities committed by the Nazis in the occupied territories was tightly controlled. Of course, the Rosanis and the Naglers still had family and friends in the devastated region and Rita and her mother had direct contact with Jewish refugees passing through the port of Trieste, but even if they had heard the rumours, they could scarcely have believed the full horror of what was happening in their homeland.

Closer to home, the first in a series of violent attacks against Jewish offices and organisations took place, culminating in a failed attempt to burn down Trieste's magnificent synagogue. Although they did not have to wear the star of David, as required elsewhere in Nazi-occupied Europe, the restrictions in place on what was left of Italy's native Jewish population were considerable.

Freedom of movement was highly curtailed. Jews had to make endless appearances before a variety of authorities and were barred altogether from certain places, including the principal vacation destinations. They were also required to annul any new surnames they had adopted in order to conceal their Jewish origins. Any distinction between loyal Italian Jews and foreigners, Zionists or anti-fascists was, by now, irrelevant. They were all judged to be members of a universal community and a threat to the Italian nation.

. . .

CASTEL FRENTANO, the small town in the province of Chieti where the Naglers were now interned, was just twenty kilometres north of Casoli. Detained in the former school and movie theatre, the people of the village opened their doors to the detainees who had been thrust upon them. Amongst the handful of foreign Jews interned along with the Naglers was Samuel Grauer, a carpenter originally from Jaroslaw in Poland, but more recently a resident of Trieste, his wife Rosa Jordan from Koenigsberg in Germany and their son Marco.

Despite the improved conditions on offer in Castel Frentano, Salo's health continued to deteriorate. He suffered from varicose veins, asthma, hypertension and shortness of breath. He may well have been suffering from malaria, but as the disease had officially been eradicated by the regime, no treatment was available to him.

By December 1941, Rita's relationship with Kubi was showing signs of strain as each continued to suffer from periodic bouts of depression. As well as the infrequency of his letters, another source of tension was Kubi's desire to leave Italy. Despite everything, Rita was determined to remain. In September 1940 she had written to Kubi:

> You know very well that I want to stay here ... I was born in
> Trieste and so I'm bound to this land.

On New Years Day 1942, perhaps following a bout of New Year reflection, Rita asked Kubi directly about his intentions after the war. She returned to the subject in a subsequent letter, asking him if he still wanted to marry her. But by the spring of 1942, their engagement was over. The strain of enforced separation had been too much for them.

Despite their separation, Rita continued to write regularly to Kubi. Reflecting on their breakup, she suggested that perhaps theirs wasn't true love after all and that it was better to have realised that now, before it was too late.

In July 1942, Trieste's synagogue was again targeted by a fascist mob. In September, Rita asked Kubi to return all her letters to her or to burn them. Kubi refused. Meanwhile in the desert of North Africa, Lieutenant-General Sir Bernard Law Montgomery was preparing to launch an audacious offensive at an Egyptian railway halt called El Alamein. The tide of war was about to turn.

Giacomo 'Kubi' Nagler (photo credit: www.campocasoli.org)

CHAPTER 8

*R*ita's letters to Kubi from 7 November 1942 to 1 June 1943 have not survived. We know, however, that on 21 November 1942 a minor miracle happened — Rita's Italian citizenship was confirmed. As Mussolini's attitude towards the Jews, increasingly inspired by Hitler, hardened and foreign Jews were being interned and deported, confirmation of her status as an Italian citizen was a potentially live-saving development.

In Trieste, antisemitic attacks continued. On 30 January 1943 the synagogue was once again attacked. On 1 February fascist squads attacked Jewish offices, shops and houses. Many Jews were injured, some seriously. On 19 May 1943, just metres from the entrance to Rita's school, fascist squads armed with hand grenades attacked Jewish shops and businesses. Considerable damage was inflicted in the looting and violence that followed.

We don't know for sure if Rita was directly caught up in these events but, in what was left of Trieste's tight-knit Jewish community, she can't have been oblivious to what was going on. On 1 June 1943, she wrote to Kubi to ask what he wanted her to do with the Nagler family property in Trieste, as she could no longer guarantee its safety.

On 15 June, Radio Roma announced that all foreign Jews in Italy were to be repatriated. At the committee of assistance, in which Rita had become increasingly active, the announcement sparked frantic activity. Under threat of deportation to Nazi Germany or Poland, desperate plans to escape to Palestine or neutral Switzerland were accelerated.

While letters to relatives in Galicia and Moravia went unanswered, news of the extermination camps had reached as far south as Ferramonti. For Italy's Jewish population, the situation was reaching a terrifying climax.

Meanwhile, the tide of war had turned. Poorly equipped and badly led, the Italian army had now suffered humiliating defeats in northern and eastern Africa and the hasty invasion of Greece had resulted in an embarrassing and costly stalemate.

On the evening of 10 July 1943, Operation Husky, the Allied invasion of Sicily, was launched. The Allies quickly established a foothold on the island. Within ten days the Allied military government had repealed any law that discriminated against a person or persons on the basis of race, colour or creed. This declaration provided a much-needed message of hope to what remained of Italy's Jewish population.

From Rome, Italy's military and political leaders looked on with growing concern. On 24 July the Fascist Grand Council approved a motion of no confidence in Mussolini. The following day Il Duce was formally relieved of office and arrested. For the Jews of Trieste, the news was met with cautious optimism. At Castel Frentano the church bells rang.

On 29 July the chief of police in Rome ordered the release

of all interned Italian Jews. On 29 August, the release was ordered of all stateless persons held at Ferramonti. With the Allied liberation of Sicily and the sudden fall of Mussolini, perhaps Rita and Kubi would survive after all.

CHAPTER 9

$\mathcal{F}$ ollowing his arrest, Mussolini was placed under house arrest, first on the island of La Maddalena, and then at the Hotel Campo Imperatore, high on the slopes of Monte Portella in the region of Abruzzo, where he remained until 12 September 1943. From here he was liberated in a dramatic glider-borne raid led by German commando Otto Skorzeny. He was then installed at the head of the new Italian Social Republic, with its centre of power at Salò, on the banks of Lake Garda.

On 8 September 1943 the armistice between Italy and the Allies had been announced. In accordance with the terms of the agreement, the Italian army ceased combat activities and its navy sailed to Allied ports to surrender. The Germans considered the armistice a betrayal and had already activated Operation Achse, the disarming, by force if necessary, of the Italian army.

Italy was subsequently divided into two shifting zones, the Nazi-occupied zone to the north and the Allied-liberated zone to the south. Unfortunately, the Nagler and Rosani families found themselves on the wrong side of the dividing line.

On 10 September, just two days after the armistice, all remaining Jews interned at Ferramonti, in the liberated southern zone, were released. Despite this welcome development the future remained uncertain for the Jews in northern and central Italy. Trieste and the surrounding area was incorporated into the *Adriatisches Kustenland*, an operational zone under Nazi control, although nominally part of the newly constituted Italian Social Republic.

For the Jews of northern Italy, the German occupation marked the beginning of a new phase of persecution. The Nazi occupation of Trieste completed the transformation of city's Jewish population from an integrated and prosperous community to a persecuted and ostracised enemy.

Fearing the worst, many Jews in northern Italy immediately began marching south towards the advancing Allies. While Rita pleaded with her parents to join the refugees heading south, Wehrmacht troops moved quickly to occupy the city.

With the country in crisis, communication between the Rosanis and Naglers became increasingly frantic. The last letter from Rita to Kubi before the German occupation was dated 4 September 1943. 'Here everything is rather hot', she observed, clearly referring to more than just the weather. After writing to him two or three times a week for the entire three years of his incarceration, the Nazi occupation of northern Italy marked the end of the correspondence between Rita and Kubi.

Meanwhile in Verona the first assembly of the new Fascist Republican Party, reconstituted on 15 September 1943, approved a manifesto which included the explicitly antisemitic declaration that:

members of the Jewish race are foreigners. During this war
they are an enemy nationality.

Specialised police units of the Gestapo section IVB4, the
Nazi Security Police (SIPO) and Security Service (SD) were
assigned the task of rounding up Italy's Jews. The Italian
headquarters of SIPO/SD was located in Verona, under the
general command of SS-Gruppenführer Wilhelm Harster.
The arrest and deportation of the Jews was overseen by
Hauptsturmführer Dannecker Theodor Dannecker (until
December 1943) and *Sturmbannführer* Friedrich Boßhammer
(from January 1944). In the *Adriatisches Küstenland*, a partially
autonomous branch of the SIPO-SD was established under
the command of Gruppenführer Odilo Globočnik. These
fanatical generals approached their task with merciless
efficiency.

ON 9 OCTOBER 1943, the day of Yom Kippur, the holiest day
in the Jewish calendar, the Einsatzkommando conducted its
first roundup of Italian Jews. Two days later the Allies intercepted a telegram from the head of the Reich Secret Service
to Obersturmbannführer Herbert Kappler, head of the SD in
Rome. The telegram simply stated:

> The Italian Jews must be immediately and completely
> eliminated.

Section IVB4 swung into action, making its first arrests
in Trieste on 9 October 1943. This was followed by a massive
roundup in Rome a week later, which resulted in the trans-
portation to Auschwitz of over a thousand Roman Jews. A
similar fate awaited the Jewish community of Florence.

In Trieste, a second roundup took place on 29 October,

and a third on 20 January 1944. Dr Carlo Morpurgo, the secretary general of the Jewish community, refused to abandon the elderly patients under his care at the Jewish *Pia Casa Gentilomo* hospice. Dr Morpurgo would die alongside his patients in the gas chambers of Auschwitz.

In total, 1,235 Jews were deported from the *Adriatisches Kustenland*, including 708 from Trieste. While the arrests and deportations had initially been conducted by German personnel, Italian fascists were soon complicit in such operations.

At the Risiera di San Sabba, previously an industrial rice-husking facility in the suburbs of Trieste, the Germans had established the only concentration camp with a crematorium on Italian soil. About 5,000 Slavs, Italian anti-fascists and Jews would be killed here, while thousands more were imprisoned, before being transported to concentration camps in the north. Between October 1943 and February 1945, 60 convoys left Trieste on their way to the extermination camps of central and eastern Europe.

By December 1943, the Nazis considered Trieste *Judenfrei*.

As Jews were being forced from Trieste, a charismatic Italian veteran of the Russian front was heading in the opposite direction. Handsome and square jawed with strong dark features and bright piercing eyes, Umberto Ricca was born in Pisa in 1899 and came from a family with a distinguished military history. At fourteen, he had been sent to the Military College in Rome. When the First World War broke out, little more than a boy, he had been sent to the Italian front at Asiago. After the war he completed further military training in Turin and served as commander of the Peloritana infantry division during the Second Italo-Abyssinian War.

By 1939, Ricca was back in Italy, serving as chief of staff of the Pasubio division, then garrisoned at Verona. In 1940, his division was posted to the French border, then to Fiume and Klana on the eastern front. In 1941 he took part in the occupation of the coastal town of Šibenik. Then, in July 1941, he was posted to the Russian front. By October 1942, he was back in Italy and spent May to July 1943 convalescing in Rome. On 25 July 1943, he assumed command of the 10th artillery regiment GAF (*Guardia alla frontiera*), stationed at Selce, in the disputed Slovenian territory. In command of a shabby, ill-equipped regiment in a precarious military situation, it was hardly a plumb posting.

By September 1943, with the armistice signed and German occupation looming, Ricca was posted to the garrison at Trieste. Irate and disillusioned, he grabbed a rifle and some hand grenades and led a patrol around the war-ravaged city. He watched on in disgust as German soldiers fired a submachine gun from the balcony of a nearby hotel. There were 40,000 men in this city, the population was on our side, why, Ricca wanted to know, were we surrendering?

Ricca raised his concerns with his superior officer, but General Giovanni Esposito, *Comando della Difesa Territoriale di Trieste*, refused to authorise resistance to the German occupation. The next day Ricca's men were forced to surrender. Whilst his men would end up in prison camps in Germany, Ricca had no intention of surrendering. Ditching his uniform, for the first time in his distinguished military career, the Colonel went absent without leave.

In need of documentation and somewhere to hide out, he remembered a musician from Trieste he had met in Rome two months earlier. He knocked on her door and, to his relief, found her at home. She invited him for lunch and he stayed for four days. After procuring false papers he made his excuses and left. He had an uncle in Venice who might just be willing to help him.

Tipped off about German checks at Mestre, the Colonel abandoned his journey to Venice at the small station at Latisana, from where he caught a bus to Lignano, a coastal resort on the Adriatic coast. The resort was teeming with Jewish refugees desperately fleeing the city. He found lodgings in a local boarding house and, amongst the many families seeking refuge in the town, he encountered three pretty young girls from Trieste. Despite the precariousness of their situation, they danced and joked together. One of them in particular caught the Colonel's eye. She was short, with coppery red hair and a fiery temperament.

Il Colonnello di S. M. Ricca

Colonel Umberto Ricca (photo credit: unknown)

CHAPTER 10

*S*omehow Rita had made it out of Trieste. As the Germans had occupied the city, she persuaded her parents to flee to one of the small fishing villages along the Adriatic coastline. Here they had found friends amongst the people of Cinto Caomaggiore. Despite the determined anti-semitic propaganda emanating from both the church and the state, and the severe reprisals for those caught sheltering fugitives, the local people treated the Jewish refugees in their midst with compassion and kindness.

Rita and the Colonel soon became friends. She confided in him that she too was on the run from the fascist authorities. Although the committee of assistance had been formally dissolved by the fascist regime, its activities had continued in the shadows. From her modest beginnings making dolls, Rita's involvement had clearly become more subversive.

As the persecution of the Jews intensified, the committee had established escape routes from central Europe, some of which passed through Italy on the way to France or neutral Switzerland. With the help of volunteers like Rita, between 5,500 and 6,000 Jews reached Switzerland. Another 500 are thought to have made the perilous journey south towards the frontline. Through these clandestine operations, Jewish volunteers experienced the value of solidarity and, in taking a stand against the regime, enjoyed a renewed sense of self-worth. But clandestine Jewish operatives were mercilessly hunted down and Rita's involvement had not gone unnoticed by the fascist authorities.

For his part, the Colonel was looking for contacts in the resistance movement. With her knowledge of the Jewish underground, perhaps Rita could help. Lacking funds and documents, his situation amongst these fugitive Jews remained precarious. Promising that he wouldn't forget about her, the Colonel once again set off towards Venice to see his uncle.

But it wasn't exactly the warm welcome he'd been hoping for that greeted him in Venice. He persuaded his uncle to part with 10,000 lire but, fearing reprisals, his elderly *zio* begged him not to return, nor even to even write to him. As he got up to leave, his uncle didn't even wave from the window.

Ricca's next stop was at the villa of Major Camillo Brena, a gentleman of some means who had served under Ricca for a few days in Verona. This time the welcome was warm, despite their ideological differences, and Ricca had no difficulty in persuading Major Brena to part with 5,000 lira, some clothing and, most significantly, the address of a good friend in Verona, a classics professor named Francesco Viviani.

MEANWHILE, the first German troops were arriving in Abruzzo. Convoys of trucks flooded into the region and troops immediately began strengthening the fortifications of the Gustav Line, the virtually impenetrable defensive wall that stretched across the Italian peninsula, from the Adriatic Sea in the east to the Tyrrhenian in the west, with the imposing medieval monastery of Monte Cassino acting as its symbolic anchor point. Field Marshall Kesselring himself passed through to inspect the fortifications that represented Rome's last line of defence against the Allied advance from the south.

Between September and October 1943, German soldiers commandeered strategically important buildings and sites across the region, confiscating essential provisions and enlisting the local population to help dig trenches and fortify artillery emplacements.

Nestled high in the mountains, Castel Frentano occupied an important strategic position on the defensive line. A Wehrmacht command post was stationed just outside the village, whose inhabitants were just about to find themselves on the frontline of the global conflict.

CHAPTER 11

$\mathcal{T}$he winter of 1943/44 was Kubi's fourth in captivity. He faced an agonising decision — stay put at Castel Frentano and hope for the best, or flee and risk capture.

While the Germans were busy fortifying their position, an embryonic resistance movement was covertly planning its response to the local Nazi incursions. When a pistol and a rucksack were stolen from a German military truck at Castel Frentano, the Germans threatened immediate and severe reprisals. The stolen items were swiftly returned and the inhabitants of the village breathed a collective sigh of relief. Just down the road at Lanciano, a group of rebels led by a Hungarian Jew named Carlo Schönheim had seized 40 rifles and a case of hand grenades.

By now rumours had reached the internees about the plight of the Jewish populations of central and eastern Europe. But still, amongst the detainees of Castel Frentano, there was a sense of denial. Details were scarce and, even so, the extermination of an entire race just seemed inconceivable. Food was also scarce and, although the Allies were

49

approaching, the swelling rivers and clawing mud had reduced their advance to a frustrating crawl, while the mountainous terrain rendered the German defensive fortifications all but impenetrable.

Although the internees could hear the distant explosions from the frontline, the advancing Allies were still some way away. With war waging all around them and without a reliable guide to navigate the treacherous mountain terrain, an escape attempt seemed futile. It would certainly have required a Herculean effort. But for Kubi and the other internees, weakened and demoralised by years in captivity, such an effort was beyond them. Besides, amongst the internees were the carpenter's children, Marco and Tito (born in captivity on 4 February 1942), the elderly, the sick and the infirm, including Kubi's father Salo, whose health had continued to deteriorate. The risk of flight was just too great.

With an impending sense of doom, the handful of interned Jews decided to stay put at Castel Frentano. In the distance, the snow-capped peaks of Monte Amaro were a reminder of happier days spent in the mountains above Trieste. They were also a clear indication of another harsh winter to come.

As the internees equivocated, Schönheim's rebels struck, seizing 250 rifles, an automatic machine gun with 1000 rounds and four cases of hand grenades. But the actions of the local resistance movement drew attention to the foreign Jews interned nearby at Castel Frentano. On 1 October 1943, an order was issued from the German military command at Ascoli Piceno, just 80 kilometres to the north. All Jews in the province were to be rounded up.

A few days later sporadic skirmishes broke out on the road to Lanciano. Schönheim's band was on manoeuvres once again. Years later the 'October heroes' of Lanciano would be recognised as one of the few significant examples of popular uprising against the Nazi occupation, while the town itself would be awarded the *Medaglia d'oro al valor militare*, for its collective response to the German occupation. For the internees, news of the revolt provided a brief glimmer of hope, perhaps even a welcome distraction in which to launch a desperate last-minute bid for freedom.

As the frontline drew ever closer, Allied artillery targeted the German positions around Castel Frentano. Kubi, Salo and Della watched on in trepidation as great convoys of German troops passed through the village on their way to the frontline. Just 35 kilometres to the south, Montgomery's Eighth Army was hammering the German position at the River Trigno. The battle raged on for a week before the Germans eventually pulled back to the Gustav Line.

At Castel Frentano the situation was increasingly tense. On 25 October 1943, the order was given to evacuate, as increasing numbers of German troops occupied strategic points in and around the village. Afraid and with nowhere to go, the interned Jews remained behind to await their fate.

With the frontline now within touching distance, this was the time to flee. But still the internees hesitated. Rumours of spies circulated. German squads active in the area were rounding up local work parties. Fortifications were strengthened. Trenches, tunnels and artillery emplacements were constructed everywhere.

Finally, loud banging on the locked doors of the village signified the arrival of the SS. Their worst fears had been realised. The internees were rounded up and led to the local primary school where they were locked in a classroom.

Seventy-two hours after detaining the internees, the Germans fell back to the Sangro, taking up the fortified positions around Castel Frentano. The interned Jews, meanwhile, were transferred to *fornace di Crocetta*, a massive disused industrial bakery with imposing brick walls and hard cold floors. They were fed occasional pieces of stale bread by the unit of Volksdeutsche guards assigned to watch over them. The guards, from the occupied territories of the Balkans, Poland and eastern Europe, were not the murderous fanatics of the Einsatzkommando, and they were curious rather than hostile towards the Jews under their guard. They shared scraps of tobacco and even a drop of wine with their prisoners.

As the Allied advance continued, the buildings of the *fornace* became a staging post for Germans evacuated from the frontline. Trucks full of injured soldiers passed through the camp. As the casualties mounted, the mood amongst the detainees darkened as they feared violent reprisals.

The internees from Castel Frentano, including Kubi, Salo and Della, as well as the Polish carpenter Samuel and his wife and their two boys, spent two long days at this cold and bleak holding station, before being transferred to the infamous POW camp at Chieti Scalo. From here, Kubi managed to smuggle out a postcard. Despite everything, he wrote that they were well and in good health.

On 11 November another postcard from Kubi made it out. It would be his last communication with the outside world.

> We're all well and hope you are too. We hope to be able to write more soon. Best wishes to all. And to our *"padrone di casa"*.
>
> Yours Salo

Although the letter was signed Salo, it was written in Kubi's distinctive hand.

On 14 November, while the Naglers were still incarcerated at the POW camp at Chieti, the manifesto of the Social Republic, the 'Carta di Verona', declared unequivocally that Jews were the enemies of the state. The declaration provided renewed moral impetus for the general deportation of all Jews from Italy.

The Naglers were held at the POW camp at Chieti until 20 November, when they were transferred by military convoy to the nearby town of L'Aquila, where they were held in a requisitioned military barracks. Castel Frentano, their home for so long, was now right on the frontline. On the night of 27/28 November, the Allies launched a ferocious attack on the Gustav Line. On 30 November, they took the village itself. It is said that the Gurkhas who led the assault on Castel Frentano that day took no prisoners. On the same day, the general deportation of all Italian Jews was announced.

DESPITE EVERYTHING, within the confines of the barracks of L'Aquila, the interned Jews were, for the time being, safe. Then, on 18 December, came the news that they had been dreading. They were to be transported north. Over Christmas 1943 the interned Jews were once again rounded up. On 13 January 1944 they were transported to the concentration camp at Villa La Selva near Florence.

After a bleak period of incarceration at the villa, on 26 January the Naglers were transported to the infamous San Vittore prison in Milan. Conditions here were appalling. Prisoners were beaten and tortured by the Gestapo. The cell walls were covered in graffiti — the curses, blessings, signatures and farewells of previous occupants. Some prisoners took their own lives, throwing themselves from the upper floors of the building. Others didn't survive the

Gestapo interrogations. One prisoner was torn to pieces by a dog.

On 30 January, the Castel Frentano internees left San Vittore, a desperate line of broken men, women and children. Even the sick were carried out on stretchers. As they made their way to the trucks that would transport them to the waiting wagons, those who remained behind shouted out blessings and farewells, offering what little they had to the departing Jews. An orange, a pair of gloves, a woollen scarf, a piece of chocolate. 'Take care', they shouted. 'Be strong!' With kicks and punches, the Jews were loaded onto the waiting lorries that would take them to Milan's central station.

At platform twenty-one they were unloaded from the trucks and forced onto the waiting wagons. It was dark and noisy. Orders were yelled and beatings administered. Fifty or sixty men, women and children were forced into each wagon. No water or light. Some straw on the floor. A bucket for excrement. Everyone was crying. Then only prayers. Then silence. For seven days they travelled like this. Twelve hundred kilometres across frozen Europe. Among them more than forty children, including Marco and Tito, the carpenter's sons. Tito's second birthday passed on that long train journey to hell.

Finally, they arrived. The silence that had paralysed the long journey from Milan was broken by the harsh shouts of the SS guards who were waiting for them on the platform.

— Wieviel stück?
— 650 stück.

Only 97 men and 31 women survived the selection process that took place on the platform at Auschwitz that day, amongst them Samuel the carpenter and his wife. For them, it was just a stay of execution. They would join slave parties, to be worked to death at a future time and place unknown.

Back on the platform, Marco and Tito, separated from their parents, were led immediately towards the gas chambers. It was 6 February 1944, Marco's fourth birthday. He took his little brother's hand and squeezed. He would never let go.

CHAPTER 12

*I*f Kubi, Salo and Della survived the train journey from Milan to Auschwitz, it is likely that they too were immediately sent to the gas chambers.

Of the precise fate of her ex-fiancé, Rita could have known little. It had been two years since she had broken up with Kubi, four months since she had last heard from him, and three months since she had met Colonel Ricca, with whom she was once again reunited.

According to the archives of the partisan movement, Rita Rosani joined the armed resistance in mid-February 1944, just days after Kubi and the others from Castel Frentano had arrived at Auschwitz. She was no longer the moody, self-absorbed girl of her youth. The depression and mood swings that she had suffered following the introduction of the racial laws seemed to be behind her. She had a new purpose in life, not the traditional 'feminine' role of a simple '*staffetta*' or messenger, but an armed combatant in the fight against the Nazi occupation.

By March 1944 Rita and the Colonel had arrived in Verona. They soon made contact with Francesco Viviani, a

Latin professor who also happened to be head of the local branch of the *Comitato di Liberazione Nazionale* (CLN), a political umbrella organisation opposed to fascism and the German occupation.

Viviani had recently returned from Agrigento, where he had been banished as an enemy of the regime. A long-standing opponent of fascism and associate of Tito Zaniboni (famous for his first failed assassination attempt against Mussolini in 1925), Viviani took a cavalier approach to his personal security. Even though Verona was now the epicentre of the Italian fascist state, the classics professor strolled the city's streets without an apparent care in the world.

Rita and the Colonel immediately warmed to him. He set them up in Isola della Scala, a small town to the south of the city, where Rita suffered a sudden bout of malaria for which she was prescribed a dose of quinine. Meanwhile, the Colonel was entrusted with the command of the military wing of the CLN. He divided the Veronese territory into five areas, delegating the command of individual units to other officers returning from the Russian front.

The partisans moved from place to place, always staying just one step ahead of the authorities. As they moved, their numbers swelled, with veterans of the Russian campaign, deserters and draft dodgers joining their ranks. A few modestly armed men and women, playing a deadly game of cat and mouse with the ruthless Nazi authorities.

Rita, her fever now passed, narrowly evaded capture at Bovolone, a few kilometres from Isola della Scala. She also helped to foil a fascist plot to ambush a safe-house in Zevio, for which she earned the rank of second lieutenant. She also acquired the *nom de guerre* Cornelia, perhaps in reference to the wife of Roman general Julius Caesar, although most of her comrades continued to call her Rita.

Then, on 14 June 1944, just days after the Allied landings at Normandy, members of the local CLN were arrested. Their security compromised, Rita and the Colonel were again forced to flee.

On 24 July news arrived that Viviani himself had been arrested, along with the entire leadership cell of the Veronese CLN. For four days the captured partisans were beaten and tortured at the city's infamous Montorio barracks. Viviani said nothing, but the fascists found a list of names of the rebels operating in the area. The Colonel's name was at the top of the list.

Abandoning the territory to the south of Verona, Rita, now elevated to the rank of *'tenente',* and the Colonel fled to the hills to the north of the city, where they rendezvoused with their comrades. From their base in Provale, in the Valpantena valley, they made contact with an underground operative known to them only as *Eugenio*.

The mysterious agent *Eugenio* was in fact Carlo Perucci, a local teacher, trade unionist and anti-fascist, who also went by the code names *Professore* and Mario. In 1936 he had graduated in literature at the University of Padova, having completed his thesis on the Sicilian dramatist and poet Luigi Pirandello. For most of his life Perucci had lived in Verona, where he taught at the prestigious Liceo Maffei school. When war broke out, he served as an infantry officer and was decorated with the silver medal for military valour. Following the armistice and occupation, he joined the resistance.

At the end of November 1943, *Eugenio* was dropped by submarine at the mouth of the River Po. Heading north towards Verona, his mission, codenamed Operation Rye, was to identify and report on the railway traffic on the Brenner line and to liaise with partisans operating in the province of

Verona. Without a radio or other means of communication, his was no easy task.

Eugenio promised Ricca weapons and false documents. Rita and the Colonel were to go to a village in Valpolicella, where they would have their photos taken for their new false papers. It was a gruelling march in a heavy storm. With broken shoes and no raincoat, Rita arrived at their destination drenched. On the return journey she was forced to abandon her broken shoes and continue the journey barefoot. Despite the ordeal and the risk of betrayal and capture at every turn, Rita was good humoured, cracking jokes and teasing the Colonel.

Back in the hills, the safe-house at Provale had been compromised. A fascist spy was said to be operating in the area and Rita and the Colonel stole away to the neighbouring settlement of Chieve. Surrounded by the forest and pastures of Monte Comune, the rebels took up residence in a remote farmhouse. They slept on two straw mattresses in the attic, while the farmer's wife, two children and a pig occupied the kitchen below. Of the weapons and munitions promised by *Eugenio*, nothing had materialised.

By now the hills of northern Verona were swarming with deserters, draft-dodgers and outlaws opposed to the German occupation, as well as elements of various fascist and Nazi brigades operating in the area. At the nearby Osteria Degani, you were just as likely to bump into a Wehrmacht infantryman as a communist partisan.

Calling themselves the *Gruppo bande armate Pasubio*, after their combat division in Russia, the partisans were organised into two bands of combatants, the 'Medusa' stationed at Monte Baldo and led by Tenente 'Fiorello' and 'L'Aquila' stationed at Monte Comune led by Tarcisio Benetti, code-named 'Rostro'.

Rita and the Colonel were attached to the second group.

Eight in total, their band included 'Selva', a veteran of the Garibaldi division who had seen action in Parma; 'Gallo', a Sicilian with a unique talent for impersonating farmyard animals — in particular the rooster, he also served as the camp cook, a role that Rita was pleased to have avoided; and Dino Degani, tall, skinny, and just 18-years-old, they called him 'Giraffa'.

Armed with 13 rifles, two sub-machine guns and 12 cases of hand grenades commandeered from a fascist weapons store, they somehow hoped to take on the might of the German Wehrmacht.

Few in number and poorly equipped they may have been, but in Colonel Ricca they had a competent and experienced leader. A respected military commander and decorated veteran of the Russian campaign, he knew how to run a combat unit. Persuasive, respectful, sometimes even paternal, he taught Rita how to strip, clean and assemble a rifle. Together they patrolled the area, gathering arms and information. Sometimes they just wandered through the quiet woodland in search of porcini mushrooms. With summer approaching, the hilltop pastures around Monte Comune filled with buttercups, wild carnations and geraniums. Despite everything, Rita and the Colonel were happy.

But in the hills and valleys around Verona, Black Brigade raids, shootings and burnings were an almost daily occurrence. The arrival of General Kesselring at nearby Recoaro Terme had intensified anti-partisan activity in the area. The Rizzardi Black Brigade, named after Count Stefano Rizzardi, a fascist volunteer killed by Slovenian partisans in the battle against Italian occupation, was preparing for its next strike against the rebel bands operating in the hills to the north of Verona.

By the beginning of September it finally seemed like the the weapons the partisans had been promised might actually materialise. First, though, they had to reach an agreement with the Brigata Avesani, a neighbouring band of partisans operating to the north. The summit between the two factions was to take place on the far side of Monte Baldo.

It would be an arduous and dangerous mission, first a 45 kilometre hike to the Bocchetta di Noale, high on the Monte Baldo ridge, then, the following day, to the rendezvous point on the far side of the mountain range. Rita, suffering from a heavy cold, was told to wait at the farmhouse. 'Be careful', the Colonel warned his comrades on the eve of the mission, issuing clear instructions to post vigilant sentry and lookout guards.

The next morning the Colonel rose early.

'I'm ready', said Rita, 'Let's go!'

'But you promised me you'd stay at home!'

'I thought you were smarter. You should have known I was joking!'

She looked up at him with her piercing blue eyes. There was nothing he could do.

WITH THEIR GUIDE, they set off along the Valpantena, the valley that would lead them to Monte Baldo. Rita was quiet as they climbed, a sure sign that she was suffering. Her matted red hair was sticking to her forehead. Perhaps she was experiencing another bout of malaria. 'How are you feeling?', the Colonel asked her. Rita gestured for him to continue.

Somehow she made it to the village of Peri, some forty kilometres north of Verona. There were Germans stationed in the village, so they crossed the river and arrived a few minutes later at Rivalta, where they searched in vain for somewhere to shelter. Even the local priest turned them away. Desperate, Ricca returned to the rectory. 'Father', he quickly explained, 'I'm a colonel with the resistance. Do you understand?' The priest opened his door and Rita immediately collapsed on the sofa.

Leaving her in the care of the priest, the Colonel set off into the hills with his guide.

HIS MISSION ACCOMPLISHED, a few days later the Colonel returned to the rectory. After a restless couple of nights, Rita was sent to Verona for further rest and recuperation. Following a short period of convalescence, she begged Ricca to allow her to return to their hideout in the hills at Monte Comune. Ricca wanted her to stay and rest another day. 'Tomorrow is the eve of Rosh Hashanah', she pleaded, 'I'd like to spend it up in the hills.'

Back at the farmhouse, eight new volunteers had joined the band, three of whom had gone to the nearby village of Grezzana on an arms run. They were expected back at any moment.

Relieved to be back in the hills with her comrades, before going to bed that night Rita recited the Shema, an ancient Hebrew prayer asking for God's protection.

CHAPTER 13

MONTE COMUNE, VERONA, 17 SEPTEMBER 1944

*I*t's 4:00 a.m. on the eve of Rosh Hashanah. Dawn has not yet broken, but Rita can't sleep. She is worried about her comrades who haven't yet returned from Grezzana.

As Rita is struggling to sleep, sixty men from two platoons of the second company *Ordine Pubblico* are assembling at their barracks. The first platoon, led by Lieutenant Alessandro Tormene, is joined by a third platoon of forty cadets from the 'B.Mussolini' youth legion, led by Mario Scaroni, a 19-year-old Second Lieutenant from Brescia. They are joined by 18 men from the *Zug Gendarmerie* (the German railway police), as well as a Marshall and eleven men from the *Fliegerabwehrkanone* (the German anti-aircraft service). All told, a force of 130 men has been assembled for the dawn raid.

At 5:00 a.m. Colonel Ricca gets up and orders three of his

men to relieve the sentries. He too is worried about the men who still haven't returned from Grezzana.

At 6:00 a.m. the three fascist platoons, armed with intelligence gleaned from the three partisans they intercepted at a trattoria in Grezzana, manoeuvre into position. While the excited youngsters of the Mussolini brigade are anxious to get involved, the veterans of the second company are more cautious.

With hostages placed in front of them, the fascist platoons advance towards the farmhouse at Monte Comune. Although they have been easily discovered, their base at Monte Comune does have certain attributes. The terrain is steep and rugged, with a possible escape route to the north.

From his sentry post, 'Gatto' spots the advancing formation. He fires off a shot, hitting one of the hostages, his cousin, in the arm. *'Allarmi!'*, he yells.

Rita wakes with a start, her red hair sticking to her sweating forehead. Wearing a wooly sweater, dark grey trousers that are too big for her and a new pair of red shoes, she grabs her rifle and ammunition and rushes outside.

Her comrades have already taken up position around the the clearing. A hundred metres away, 'Giraffa' is firing from his Sten gun. The fascists return fire. Bullets whistle overhead. Without hesitation, Rita loads her rifle and fires.

For ten minutes the partisans resist. But, surrounded, they soon run out of ammunition. Finally, the order is given to retreat. 'Move out! Run! Run! Out! Out! Out!'

Under covering fire, the partisans withdraw.

But Rita doesn't move. 'Rostro' approaches her. 'Let's go!', he yells. 'I've spent my last cartridge.'

There are just a few of them left in the middle of the field behind the farmhouse. 'Rostro', with his machine gun slung over his shoulder, sets off towards the slope, but still Rita doesn't move.

The Colonel appears at her side and grabs her by the shoulder.

'Come on!', he shouts. 'We can't stay here!'

'I can't do it anymore', she cries.

'Come on!' he urges her. 'One more push!'

He takes her by the shoulder as bullets zing overhead.

'I've been hit!' she exclaims.

He freezes.

'Where? Let me see.'

'Here on my side.'

'Let's go! If not they'll get you.'

He drags her a few metres towards the slope. Another hail of bullets whizzes past them. She screams. 'I'm hit again! I'm finished.'

In the confusion that follows, Rita is left behind. 'Giraffa' rushes to her aid, but he too is hit and falls prone to the ground beside her.

Second Lieutenant Mario Scaroni advances towards the fallen rebels. Lieutenant Tormene is not far behind him.

'I surrender', Rita manages to mutter.

Scaroni raises his gun and fires.

AFTERWORD

On 20 March 1948 a sombre ceremony took place in Piazza Brà. Umberto Terracini, the Jewish president of the Constituent Assembly, the parliamentary body responsible for restoring Italian democracy, pinned a gold medal to the chest of a crying mother. Among the many dignitaries present that day, a handsome colonel in the uniform of the Italian parachute regiment.

Homeless and out of work, his homeland destroyed, his adopted hometown of Trieste now alien to him, for Ludwig Rosenzweig the loss of his only daughter had been too much to bear. He died, it is said, of a broken heart on 27 February 1947.

The grieving mother would never recover from the traumatic events that befell her family during those long years of persecution and war. On 1 May 1954, she suffered a fatal brain haemorrhage and was buried alongside her husband at the Jewish cemetery in Trieste. For decades, their gravestones were tended to by a family from Cinto Caomaggiore who had sheltered them during the war.

After the death of Rita, Colonel Umberto Ricca was sheltered in Milan by Clara Tadini Ferrazzi, a widow from a prominent Milanese family, who became his lifelong companion. After the war he continued his military career until he discovered Marxism in the early 1950s and decided to leave the army to undertake studies in the philosophy of science. In 1956 he joined the Italian Communist Party. His memoirs, which include his recollection of that fateful day in September 1944, were published in 1969. He died in the quiet hilltop town of Ortonovo in 1982.

After his capture in the summer of 1944, the classics professor Francesco Viviani spent time in Verona's notorious Scalzi prison before being transferred to the concentration camp at Bolzano. He was subsequently transported to Auschwitz and from their to Buchenwald. In April 1945, as the liberating Allies were approaching, the Germans issued an order to evacuate the camp. Viviani was ordered to move but, gravely ill, he couldn't. He was shot in the head by an SS guard. A piazza in Verona now bears his name, as well as an unassuming caffè in the corner of the square.

After the war Second Lieutenant Mario Scaroni was sentenced to 24 years for military collaboration. He was absolved of the murder or Rita Rosani on the grounds of insufficient evidence. Under the terms of the Togliatti Amnesty, named after the communist Minister of Justice, sentences for crimes committed during the war by both fascists and partisans were either pardoned or reduced. The amnesty commuted death sentences to life imprisonment, life imprisonment to 30 years and all other sentences above five years were reduced by two thirds. For Scaroni, this meant that his 24-year sentence was reduced to just eight. On release he moved to Umbria, where he worked as a surveyor. He died in the 1990s.

For his part in the summary execution of Dino 'Giraffa' Degani, Lieutenant Tormene was sentenced in absentia to 30 years. He had also been implicated in the murder of a British army officer at Grezzana and was taken from Verona to Bologna to be tried by the British authorities. He was found not guilty and released.

In Verona, Rome and Trieste there are streets named after Rita Rosani. In Verona, a primary school and a secondary school bear her name. At the Jewish school in Trieste, where she briefly taught, a plaque commemorates her life.

At Monte Comune, a memorial stone was erected to mark the spot where Rita Rosani and Dino Degani were killed. Every year a commemorative ceremony is held by the *Volontari della Libertà*, in collaboration with the municipal authorities of Negrar and Grezzana.

At the entrance to the Synagogue of Verona, a plaque with a passage from the Hebrew Tanakh honours Rita Rosani and the sacrifice she made 'for the highest ideals of humanity'.

NOTES

CHAPTER 2

1. In the present day Czech Republic.
2. Because of its strategic position between Italy, Hungary and Croatia, and its deep-water port, Fiume has always been a fiercely contested city, changing rulers and demographics many times over the centuries. When Salo Nagler passed through at the beginning of the twentieth century, Rijeka (as the city is known in Croatian) was enjoying a period of great prosperity, rapid economic growth and technological advancement, becoming the main maritime outlet for Hungary and the eastern part of the Austro-Hungarian empire.
3. Morris (2001), p. 30

CHAPTER 3

1. The region of Galicia is now divided between modern day Poland and the Ukraine.
2. Stanisławów, renamed Stanislav after the Soviet invasion of 1939 and called Stanislau by the German occupiers, is about 120 kilometres southeast of Lviv, the capital of eastern Galicia. Today it is Ukrainian and is known as Ivano-Frankivsk.
3. On the eve of the Second World War, Lviv (Polish: Lwów; German: Lemberg) was a multicultural city with a population of just over 300,000. In the inter-war period it was part of the Polish state, though its status was always highly contested. Ethnic Poles constituted just over 50 percent of the city's population, Jews 32 percent and Ukrainians 16 percent. Today it is Ukrainian and the city's Jewish population numbers about 5,000.

CHAPTER 4

1. In 1919 Pietro Jacchia had been amongst the very first founders of Italian Fascism in Milan. In October 1922, he participated in the 'March on Rome', before beginning to distance himself from the movement. He officially resigned from the Fascist Party in 1925. In 1931, he emigrated to Holland and in 1936 to the United Kingdom, where he mixed in resis-

tance circles of exiled Italians. Later that year he went to Spain, where he fought with the Republicans against Franco and fascist troops from Italy and Germany. He died in combat on 14 January 1937.

2. The attack on Padova's synagogue occurred on the night between 1-2 November 1926. Following a failed attempt on Mussolini's life, a squad of about 50 fascists attacked and damaged the city's principal synagogue and a smaller nearby temple. The last known attack of a Jewish synagogue had occurred in Trieste almost 50 years earlier, when the city was still part of the Austrian empire.

CHAPTER 5

1. The office of Podestà was an unelected mayor figure, appointed by the fascist party with extensive legislative and executive powers.
2. Between 1925 and 1927, the Fascist government had, in any case, dissolved opposition parties and unions.

CHAPTER 7

1. Rachele Mussolini (née Guidi) was in fact Mussolini's second wife, commonly known in Italy as Donna [Lady] Rachele.
2. On 20 January 1942, the plan to exterminate the Jews of Europe, by now already well under way in central Europe, was formalised at the SS guesthouse on the Wannsee lake near Berlin.

SELECT BIBLIOGRAPHY

Berger, Sara (editor), *I signori del terrore, Polizia nazista e persecuzione antiebraica in Italia (1943-1945)*, Cierre edizione/IVrR, 2016

Catalan, Tullia, "The Ambivalence of a Port-City. The Jews of Trieste from the 19th to the 20th Century", in Modernity and the Cities of the Jews, eds. Cristiana Facchini, Quest. Issues in Contemporary Jewish History. Journal of Fondazione CDEC, n.2 October 2011

Fargion, Liliana Picciotto, *Il Libro Della Memoria: Gli Ebrei Deportati Dall'italia (1943-1945)*, Mursia, 1992

Gilbert, Martin, *Holocaust Journey, Travelling in Search of the Past*, Weidenfeld & Nicholson, 1997

Hametz, Maura, "Zionism, Emigration, and Antisemitism in Trieste: Central Europe's 'Gateway to Zion,' 1896–1943," *Jewish Social Studies*, volume. 13, no. 3 (Spring/Summer 2007): 103–134

Hibbert, Christopher, *Benito Mussolini, A Biography*, The Reprint Society Ltd, 1963

Lorenzetti, Andrea, *Prigioniero dei Nazisti, Libero Sempre,*

Lettere da San Vittore e da Fossoli marzo-luglio 1944, A cura di Guido Lorenzetti, Mimesis, 2017

Moehrle, René, *"Fascist Jews in Trieste: social, cultural and political dynamics 1919-1938"*, in *Italy's Fascist Jews: Insights on an Unusual Scenario, eds. Michele Sarfatti, Quest. Issues in Contemporary Jewish History. Journal of Fondazione CDEC, n.11 October 2017*

Morris, Jan, *Trieste and the Meaning of Nowhere*, Faber and Faber, 2001

Pohl, Dieter, *Hans Krueger and the Murder of the Jews in the Stanislawow Region (Galicia)*, Shoah Resource Center, The International School for Holocaust Studies

Ricca, Umberto, *Tromba in fa*, Vangelista, 1969

Sarfatti, Michele, *The Jews in Mussolini's Italy: From Equality to Persecution*, The University of Wisconsin Press, 2006

Sirovich, Livio Isaak, *"Non era una donna, era un bandito", Rita Rosani, una ragazza in guerra*, Cierre Edizioni, 2014

Memoriale della Shoah di Milano, *Testimonianze di Liliana Segre*, www.memorialeshoah.it, accessed 22 February 2021

Zangarini, Maurizio, *Verona Fascista*, Istituto Veronese per la storia della resistenza, 1993

Zangarini, Maurizio, *Storia della Resistenza veronese*, Istituto Veronese per la storia della resistenza, 2012

ACKNOWLEDGMENTS

I am most grateful to Livio Isaak Sirovich, whose book, *"Non era una donna, era un bandito", Rita Rosani, una ragazza in guerra,* does a remarkable job of piecing together Rita, Kubi and Ricca's lives from various first hand sources, including the correspondence between Rita and Kubi, which I have drawn on extensively to tell this story. Without his generosity, knowledge and expertise, I would not have been able to tell this story.

Most of the correspondence referred to in this book was provided by Gianfranco Moscati to Livio Isaak Sirovich. This, along with other correspondence he discovered, is deposited and digitised in the library of the *Istituto Veronese Per La Storia Della Resistenza* in Verona. The translations of Rita's correspondence and all other translations are my own.

All the documents relating to Kubi Nagler were given by Rosetta Weintraub (whose family received them in Castel Frentano in 1943 from the Naglers after their arrest) to Isaak

Sirovich, who sent them to John Hoenig, in whose archive they are now preserved.

Much of the dialogue between Rita and Colonel Ricca has been translated in good faith from his memoirs, *Tromba in fa*, published in 1969.

I am most grateful to Professor John M. Hoenig, Jakob 'Kubi' Nagler's second cousin, who generously reviewed my manuscript and provided helpful clarification along the way.

I would also like to thank Stewart Macdonald, Professor Jeffrey Hyman and Ewen Smith. They each provided invaluable feedback and encouragement as I grappled with the story of wartime Verona. Thanks also to Neil Stewart and Anthony Wright for reviewing the manuscript and providing helpful and thoughtful feedback.

Thanks also to Professor Philippe Sands, whose work in the fields of literature and human rights are a source of inspiration. His links with Lviv (or Lemberg as he prefers to call it) are well documented, and I am most grateful for his kind words of encouragement.

Thanks also to Tobias Jones, who is another valued source of inspiration and insight. I'm grateful to him for his support and encouragement.

Finally, thanks to my number one fan in Holmfield, for her unfailing love and support. xxx

ABOUT THE AUTHOR

Richard Hough has lived in Verona since September 2011 and writes about the region's history, football, wine and culture. He is the editor of the Crazy Faithful fanzine and Notes from Verona, a collection of diary entries from inside locked down Italy. He is currently working on his next work of non-fiction, a trilogy about wartime Verona.

ALSO BY RICHARD HOUGH

Notes from Verona

Printed in Great Britain
by Amazon

63859101R00051